Let

MW01100629

SCHOOL PUBLISHERS

Photos:
Cover, © Harcourt Index; p. 2, © Harcourt Index; p. 3, © PunchStock Headquarters; p. 4, Superstock; p. 5, © PunchStock Headquarters; p. 6, © Harcourt Index; p. 7, © Corbis; p. 8, © Superstock

Printed in China

ISBN 10: 0-15-358361-4
ISBN 13: 978-0-15-358361-2

Ordering Options
ISBN 10: 0-15-358355-X (Grade K Below-Level Collection)
ISBN 13: 978-0-15-358355-1 (Grade K Below-Level Collection)
ISBN 10: 0-15-360614-2 (package of 5)
ISBN 13: 978-0-15-360614-4 (package of 5)

4 5 6 7 8 9 10 0940 15 14 13 12 11 10 09

†